THE WORLD AROUND ME
Claire Beltz

TITLE: The World Around Me-Young Leaders In The Making

AUTHOR: Claire M Beltz

WEBSITE www.clairebeltz.com.au

The moral rights of Claire Beltz to be identified as the author of this work have been asserted in accordance with the Copyright Act 1968.

First published in Australia 2017.

Any opinions expressed in this work are exclusively those of the author and are not necessarily the views held or endorsed by the publisher.

All rights reserved. No part of this publication may be reproduced or transmitted by any means, electronic, photocopying or otherwise, without prior written permission of the author.

All of the information, techniques, skills and concepts contained within this publication are of the nature of general comment only, and are not in any way recommended as individual advice. The intent is to offer a variety of information to provide a wider range of choices, now and in the future, recognising that we all have widely diverse circumstances and viewpoints. Should any reader choose to make use of the information herein, this is their decision, and the author and publisher/s do not assume any responsibilities whatsoever under any conditions or circumstances. The author does not take responsibility for the business, financial, personal or other success, results or fulfilment upon the readers' decision to use this information. It is recommended that the readers obtain their own independent advice.

National Library of Australia Cataloguing-in-Publication entry

A catalogue record for this book is available from the National Library of Australia

Beltz, Nkandu, Publisher

Title: The World Around Me-Young Leaders In The Making

(Paperback)

Subjects: Success–Anecdotes. Self-realization in Youth

Published by Nkandu Beltz

DEDICATION

Dedicated to all the young people around the world, especially 8 to 15 year olds who dream big and want to change the world, because we can.

ACKNOWLEDGEMENTS

I would like to thank Nkandu Beltz, my amazing mother, for helping me with this book. I would like to thank Jack Delosa for the inspiration to follow my dream and for writing UnProfessional (2014), which has given me many ideas as to how to run my own business. I would like to thank Helen Witting, the editor of this book. I would also like to thank the graphic designer for making it look totally cool.

I would like to thank my sister Michelle and my brother Erik Jr, both of whom I love so much. I would also like to thank my Dad, Dr Erik Beltz, for being so cool and loving and always encouraging me to do what I love and to just be me. He believes in me and usually lets me do anything I want to do.

I would like to thank my best friends Katelyn, Breanna, Emily and Angela for being such great friends and so much fun to be around.

I would like to thank my teachers at the Holy Trinity Lutheran School for encouraging me to write, especially Mr. Gork, for always listening to my ideas, and Mrs. Friberg, for encouraging me to enter writing competitions.

Most importantly, I would like to thank you, the reader, for buying this book. I hope you will enjoy reading it as much as I did writing it.

Thank you.
Claire Beltz

FOREWARD

*"There is something you must always remember.
You are braver than you believe,
Stronger than you seem
And smarter than you think."*
Winnie The Pooh

INTRODUCTION

This book is my way of expressing who I think I am. In the following chapters I talk about the obstacles I have overcome in my life and how I dealt with them. This book was written to tell you that you don't have to be afraid to do what you love. As a child I have always kept the things I love a secret because I thought they were too embarrassing to share. However, when I started expressing myself everything started to fall into place and I felt more complete. My message to you, dear reader, is: don't worry what others think of you, just follow your dreams.

A PERSONAL NOTE FROM THE PUBLISHER

To the reader,

As the Founder, Director and CEO of AscendSmart Publishing, I make it part of my practice to offer you a personal review of the authors we publish. The reason is to give you a deeper understanding of what this book is about and the impact it will have on your life.

Claire is my daughter and one of the most amazing people I know. I have been inspired by the resilience and determination that she has shown to bring this book to life so she can share with you some ideas on making the most out of your business ideas and life. You will discover just how powerful you are and that you too can succeed at anything you put your mind to.

I hope you will enjoy this read as much as I did and wish you all the success with your life and business.

With Love, Nkandu

xoxo

CHAPTER 1

How family affects your life more than it seems to

*"Role models are only of limited use.
For no-one is as important, potentially powerful and
as key in your life and world as you."*

Rasheed Ogunlaru

How I go through life

I was born in 2005 in a small country town called Kununurra, it was my hometown for quite a while. Kununurra is a small remote town in the East Kimberley, Western Australia, with only about 7500 people. My family and I lived there for 7 years. The last time I was in Kununurra was 2012 when we were moving to Victoria.

Some of my earliest memories of Kununurra are of my 6th birthday party and the year I spent in Kindergarten. Most fun memory was making a butterfly birthday cake with my mum.

I also remember Kindergarten where my teacher was a magician. She always surprised us with all kinds of tricks that I unfortunately couldn't repeat in front of my friends and siblings. The many blue tongue lizards I saw there were initially a bit scary but a grew to like them a lot. There were a lot of places around town to visit like Ivanhoe Crossing and Lake Argyle.

Growing up in Kununurra was fun because our neighbours were our friends. We loved the area so much. We were living opposite a park with a lot of grass to play on and a small playground. I learned how to ride a bike there.

Most of the time, my siblings were helpful and supportive in the things I wanted to learn and achieve, like swimming, bike riding and playing games. We were young and free, so we could be crazy as kids and have lots of fun.

I felt at home because everybody was so friendly, especially on special days like birthdays or other celebrations, like the Teddy Bear Picnic and the Diamond Dig, it felt like I was part of a big family.

If I could rate Kununurra as a place to live, it would be a high rating indeed because it is a beautiful town where I enjoyed living for most of my life.

During Holidays, we travelled to different destinations outside Australia and different areas within the country. I have seen a lot of Australia in my 11 years as well as many different other countries.

I remember so many good things from those experiences. One time we went to the Blue Mountains and stayed in a treehouse. There were lots of native birds and some fed out of my hands. It has been really fun travelling the world, seeing exciting things to tell my friends about, whilst doing my best to tell them what it would be like if they were there too. Although the world is full of amazing creations, my favourite landmark would be a tour my Dad and siblings took in Garmisch-Partenkirchen in Germany near the Austrian border.

It was raining and we were walking partly through caves and water was dripping down everywhere. We were walking next to a fast-flowing river full of waterfalls.

I may seem like a quiet person who often passes by unnoticed, but when my family and I go travelling, I always want to be in the lead. We often go climbing through hills and mountains and I'm always the first to reach the top! I like to think of myself as the quiet adventurer. But when I am with people I am really comfortable around, such as my friends or family, I really talk a lot!

Background

My mum was born in Zambia, in a small country town called Katete. She is so proud of her African heritage and she talks about it every day. My mum has a big family, and our heritage goes all the way through Southern Africa. What I know from my African grandmother's side is that my great grandmother is from Zimbabwe and my great grandfather has Mozambiquean heritage. From my

grandfather's side, I know that my great grandfather's background is Congolese DRC, but he is Zambian. My mother spent a lot of time in Botswana, which is where my older sister Michelle was born.

We visited Botswana and Zambia in 2008, when I was two and a half years old. I don't remember much about this trip, but we have a lot of photos.

The land is beautiful and that area, in the southern part of Africa, has a lot of wildlife such as Lions, Zebras, Antelopes, Elephants and more.

Whenever we look at those photos, Mum mentions all the entrepreneurs you see on the streets of Zambia and Botswana, where there are lots of businesses everywhere. Most people in those countries do not rely on government jobs, which Mum says has to do with the economy. I will talk about entrepreneurs later on in the book.

My father is Dutch; his family is of Dutch and German heritage. So I have the best of both worlds because I'm surrounded by different cultures from very different places. I'm exposed to several languages (such as English, Dutch and Bemba), food, different styles of dress and cultural celebrations.

THE WORLD AROUND ME

I love the fact that my parents keep their traditions. I like the celebration of Dad's culture; for example, on the 5th of December we celebrate 'Sinterklaas'. It's like Christmas but just a bit early. It's a celebration of good behaviour in kids over the past year. We get  presents (of course, officially only when you have been good …) and promise to be good for the coming year. But seriously… we are just kids and do what kids do. So we're not always good! Then on the 25th of December we celebrate Christmas and get more presents!

I love the fact that we get to travel the world and visit our families in very different places. What I have noticed during these travels is how people do business. That is why I thought I'd do a bit more research on entrepreneurship and how the world around me is evolving so fast.

My grandfather has a shop selling groceries. One of my uncles has an insurance business, one aunt runs a Safari Company and another uncle buys and sells cars. My mum is also an entrepreneur in the service business, helping people achieve their goals. She reads plenty of books about these topics which I can study afterwards to learn for myself.

Identity

I feel like I am a combination of so many things, which my mum compared to the 'Heinz Soup', seven veggies with golden herbs. If in  life you were put in categories, I'd be in the unknown. I've always wondered where I belong and what I could do but now I realised that I don't need a category because I'm Claire Beltz. I belong in the 'Claire Beltz' category and that shows I'm unique no matter how weird that sounds.

In my lifetime, I want to be able to travel the world, for example to California, and help and inspire as many people as I can. I will also enjoy its beautiful environment, which I've read about online. After that, I would also love to go to Los Angeles, knowing about all the business opportunities there. Of course, there are plenty of other nice places to go to, where my parents won't be able to tell me what to do.

CHAPTER 2

How change makes things both better and worse

"Sometimes the right path is not the easiest one."
Grandmother Willow (Pocahontas)

I like this quote, as I know that my path in life can be sunshine and rainbows and everything could be just right, but I also know that every now and then I might have a few hurdles, which I will learn to overcome. Finance may be a major one, but a lot of great teachers like Dr John Demartini and Jack Delosa have spoken about following your passion and the money will follow.

What I really want to do in this life is what I love, and get paid doing that. Mum always asks us, "What problems will you solve when you grow up?" This inspires me to think about what I really want to focus on. The world has a lot of problems and challenges, but we also have the potential to find solutions and overcome them.

Kids have brilliant ideas to fix some of the world's problems. There are many programs around the world helping kids like me come with solutions for the future. One is called STEMSEL, which stands for Science, Technology, Engineering, Maths, and Social Enterprise Learning. At the STEMSEL Club, young people are taught how to code. The team works with a number of scientists and university volunteers to teach kids how to make simple things like thermostats. Some kids have created talking robots and replicas of solar traffic lights. These kids have a great interest in creating a better future because there are a lot of things that will affect us as we grow older. We can be involved in many forms of change for good, such as finding ways to slow down the process of global warming, or making sure that each child has access to a good education.

I have seen my mother with her projects and she is very adaptable. I've learnt from her that things will always change in life, but the most important thing is how we react to change.

When we moved from Kununurra to Horsham in country Victoria, that was a big change. We had to learn to like our new environment.

We had a new school and had to make new friends. Our 'after school' activities changed and our whole routine was different. We had to adjust. Even though we've travelled a lot and experienced so many different places, moving to a different town is disruptive, to say the least.

My Mum is sometimes like an army commander! She says things like: "Keep your eyes on the ball. You are here to learn and have an experience."

I remember reading a book about Dr John Demartini, called *The Boy who Barked*, by Liliane Grace (2008), which I found on Mum's bookshelf.

The book is about a young boy who must deal with his twisted foot and a teacher who criticized him, calling him an unsuccessful boy who would never achieve anything.

He was 14 at the time and decided to run away from his problems and set out across America to pursue his dream. During this journey he discovers his own inner wisdom.

That young boy is now Dr John Demartini, one of today's most inspirational speakers, authors and teachers.

It is very important to have a vision of what you want your life to look like. I'm not sure what I will be when I grow up but one thing that I know is that I want to make a difference. I will be an entrepreneur and I will be solving some of the world's problems.

It is very important to have a vision of what you want your life to look like. I'm not sure what I will be when I grow up but one thing that I know is that I want to make a difference. I will be an entrepreneur and I will be solving some of the world's problems.

CHAPTER 3

About the world we've created

"Remember, you're the one who can fill the world with sunshine."
Snow White (Snow White and the Seven Dwarves)

On my travels, I have noticed that the various environments I have visited are sometimes severely polluted with rubbish. One time I was walking with my family along the bridges of the Seine in Paris near the Eiffel Tower. Paris is a very amazing and beautiful place, I was very glad to go to although on one occasion, on a cold but bright sunny day, I noticed quite a bit of rubbish along some streets.

I had similar experiences along some of the beaches and streets in Bali, Indonesia, which was surprising as Bali is one of my favourite destinations for a holiday, very rich in culture and beautiful surroundings. Most of the places we visited were very clean.

Seeing all those beautiful places, advertised as perfect, but being polluted, always fills me with sadness.

"Be part of the solution not the pollution."
The Fresh Quotes

Good people around the world can help clean up places like those I've described and for example the Government request in Rwanda for 1 day a year a complete clean up in every corner of the country.

If we stop the pollution, the world will be beautiful again. Anyone can put on some gloves and get rid of any rubbish they see. That's one important way you can help save the planet. Another way to help (and also reduce your power bills) is to install solar panels. This is a renewable energy source and using solar power instead of coal, which is a major contributor of air pollution, can make this world healthier.

There are many other ways you can help the planet and reduce pollution:

- Try not to buy things in plastic bags.
- Turn off the electricity as much as you can.
- Don't throw away food that can be reused or is still edible.
- Instead of buying water, refill your water bottles.
- When at the beach do not throw your rubbish near or in the sea, but put it in a bin.

This earth is overpopulated. It can only comfortably hold up to 4 billion people, but there are now 7 billion of us. If we want to keep the world healthy, and humans healthy too, we need to care about our land more and one way is for people to eat less meat. This is because the food and water needed to grow a cow and put its meat

THE WORLD AROUND ME

on our plates is many, many more times than used for farming fruits and veggies.

Looking after the world will also help businesses. If you are wondering how, first of all, electricity bills will go down, so businesses will save money, as stated before if we use clean and renewable energy, for example solar panels, this will help the world and you have lower electricity bills.

As a young person with my life ahead of me, I want my future to involve living in a healthy world. If we don't protect it now, we will lose our world and future generations will have a much harder time living in it, fixing the problems they will inherit. This sounds crazy to you but it's what I believe! So, let's save this world and make a difference! I believe we can all do it if we train our minds to focus on doing the very best that we can.

For example, taking shorter showers, eating more veggies instead of meat or biking to school if you live close by or walking with your friends. Other things you can do is turn off the water when you are brushing your teeth and switch off the lights when you leave the room. Make 'Earth Hour' everyday.

CHAPTER 4
Make Products that Sell

"It seemed like one should try to make the world a better place because the inverse makes no sense. The only thing that makes sense to do is strive for greater collective enlightenment."
Elon Musk

My parents have many friends who run businesses and some of my family members have their own businesses too. I find this very exciting. My parents both have businesses as well; they are both self-employed. My Dad is the coolest doctor and Mum is a social change maker. She also writes books and speaks on stage. Books about business also surround us on the many bookshelves we have throughout our house.

THE WORLD AROUND ME

When I read one of the books by Jack Delosa called 'Unprofessional', I was interested in what he talks about regarding having quality products or services for your customers. He explains that once you have a world-class service, people will buy from you. Take my sister for example; she sometimes talks about becoming an actor or a singer, but in most of our conversations the topic will go towards her becoming a doctor like Dad. What I have noticed about Michelle is that she is always practising what she loves, which is art and music. She makes sure she learns her craft so she can deliver world-class service. She has won a few awards for her arts projects and she is a very talented pianist too. She works hard at it. She once asked Dad if she could help him at the clinic, but he said no. Still, because one day she may want to become a doctor, whenever she gets a chance to use Dad's stethoscope she will listen to our heartbeats.

The secret is being the best in whatever you decide to do with your life.

My brother is a classic example of a boy who loves electronics. He wants to be a gamer. So he plays a lot of games but he also wants to  start making games so that he can sell them. He loves it. Now that my sister is learning how to code, she will teach my brother and one day he can make his own apps or games. Sir Richard Branson says that all kids should learn to code. He explains that coding is very important, so that instead of us just being consumers of technology, we can also learn to be its' creators. My sister is learning about coding through STEMSEL, which I mentioned previously. Mum mentors kids in this program and

Michelle has shown interest in the project too.

Based on my observations, it seems that a lot of people and businesses are currently creating world-class products. Take Apple, for example. We love Apple products because they are easy to use and you can sync them to other devices as well. It's a great example of a world-class product.

What world-class product will you create?

My Dad is also another example of a person creating a world-class product. He is nice to his patients and he makes sure they are treated well when they walk into his clinic. He is so good at his job that he gets a lot of gifts from his patients. This shows that he has created a successful business and is providing an important and valuable service.

If you are a kid my age, and want to start a business, if you decide to sell reused items, you should make sure they are in good condition. Or you can make your own items. Some of the kids in my town make bath salts and bath bombs to sell at the markets. One girl I know makes candles in her mum's kitchen and donates some of the money she makes to a charity. She sells her products at the local markets. These products are so good and yet she is a kid only a year older than me.

What will you make that will change the world?

CHAPTER 5

Believe in Yourself

*"Fairy tales can come true.
You gotta make them happen, it all depends on you."*
Tiana (Princess and the Frog)

One of the things we get taught at school is to have faith. You have to believe that your business will work but you also need to have a plan to make it work. If within the first few months you are struggling, it may be time to change your plan. Talk to your family and friends about it. They could help you.

If you don't have enough money to start your business, your parents might invest in your idea, but you have to make sure you own the company yourself.

If you don't believe in your idea and that it will make a difference, maybe it's not good enough. You might think up a better idea that will be more successful.

Never ever give up on your dreams. Last night on SBS we saw a program about Einstein and how hard he worked on one of his theories. It took him years, and he believed in his ideas even if it took a long time to see results. He was a clever man and he also knew that if he needed, he could ask for help from his friend Marcel Grossmann who was great at mathematics. Einstein was great at physics and he would spend a lot of time working in that field. Even when things got hard for him, he believed in his ideas and kept working on them until he eventually got the formula on how to measure the speed of light right and other amazing things that involve hard work and dedication.

What idea will you work on?

When you look at the people who are performing at the Olympics, you can see that they have worked so hard for so many years to get there. They believed in themselves, and someone else also believed in them and told that they could make it.

What do you believe you can do?

And what do others believe you can do?

Mum always says "You have so much power within you, go on and unleash your brilliance". You have to believe that you are good enough, and that you are smart enough, but you also have to be realistic and accept that you will make mistakes, which you will learn from, and move on.

I mentioned the book, *The Boy who Barked*, about Dr John Demartini, earlier which describes his life when he was a little boy. He could not walk properly and his third grade teacher told his parents that he was not smart and that he would never read or write. John believed his teacher. This meant he failed most of his school subjects. However, he was smart enough to hang out with smart kids. When he was in his teenage years, John met someone who told him that he was smart. John believed him, and this inspired him to further his education. John now runs a global education institute and he travels the world, teaching people to live an inspired life and do what they love. John believed in himself. So even if people call you names and tell you that you are not smart enough, think about the great people in this world. Be careful of believing what others say about you. You need to believe what is true for you.

CHAPTER 6
Relax and Enjoy Life

*"I know every mile will be worth my while.
I would go most anywhere to feel like I belong."*
Hercules

I am 11 years old. You might be younger or slightly older than me. As kids, we need to have fun. Yes, we need to plan for our future, but having fun is also a serious business. I remember mum picking my sister, brother and myself up from school and Erik asked mum how Leonard Cohen died. Mum said it was probably old age. I was very shocked by this. I realised that old age can kill people. She then explained that as you get old, things in your body start to slow down. She said that why it's important to play. Playing sports, as well as having friends and eating healthy food, adds years to your life. Most importantly, Mum says, you must have fun.

So how can we make life fun and still have a great future? Well, you should do whatever you like to do. I like reading books and hanging out with my friends. I also enjoy playing lots of sports at school. I even gave modelling a go. At the age of 10 years old, I was the youngest model to take part in the Tanya Powell Modelling Graduation, in December 2015. The tall, beautiful, older girls intimidated me a little bit, but I had fun, and lots of it!

My best friends and I like to play dress up. We put on mini concerts and we let our families watch our shows. They clap and cheer for us. We are making memories and we love it.

I watch my parents do what they do for a living. My Dad loves working as a medical doctor. Every time we go out, people want to talk to him. Mostly they thank him for his help. He sometimes spends hours at the hospital even during the night to make sure his patients are ok. He never complains, because he loves his job.

Can you imagine doing a job that you love and having fun with it?

It is very possible to do what you love and get paid to do it.

Mum does the same too. She is a speaker and she likes to host high teas for young people and teach them about personal development. It looks like fun! She gets to dress up and meet lots of people. Mum is always laughing on stage and she says that her job is great because she gets paid to do what she loves.

How can you get paid to do something that you love?

The key is to do what you love, and find a way of helping people while having fun.

CHAPTER 7

THE POWER OF WORDS!!!

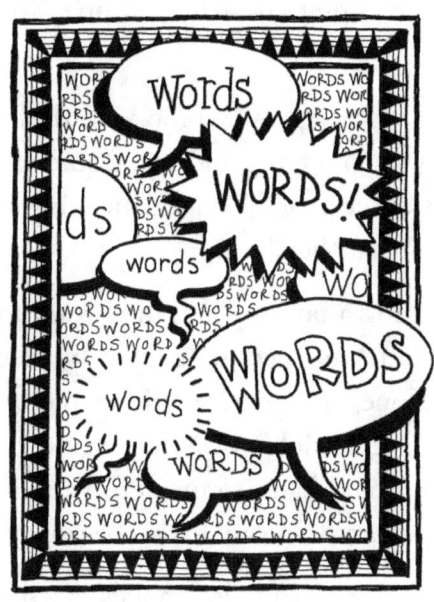

"A little consideration, a little thought for others, makes all the difference."
Eeyore, Winnie the Pooh

Words are very powerful. I always try to be careful with what I say around people. Sometimes, we can break people with words. Sometimes, it's not so much what you say but what you don't say.

When you say something bad to a person, it will make them feel bad, and they will get upset. Your friendship with them might even be broken.

Words can also help other people. Good words are very important. We need to be very encouraging and make sure we use our words to build yourself and other people's confidence, inspiring whoever you can for them to do what they love.

When you are running a business, it's important to always use good words. If you have a team, encourage them by using good words. If you are working alone, use good words to motivate yourself, like: "I am doing quite a great job", or "That was incredible" and even, "Would you look at that, I had a tonne of fun and I'm very grateful of that", but most importantly: "I can do this because I am phenomenal".

This also applies to what you say on social media. I never write anything mean on my Instagram account. Besides, if I did and Mum found out, she would probably delete the account before sitting me down and talking to me about how and why I did what I did that was wrong.

As a kid who runs a business, you can't afford to use bad words. Your business depends on it.

I remember my young brother Erik going for a play date with his friend. Erik is only eight. After a few hours, he Skyped mum on his iPad. He asked her to pick him up. Mum said ok and brought him back home.

Mum is the kind of person who will not force you to do anything, unless it has something to do with vegetables. Then she will make you eat them! Even trying to gag won't work. She made me sit at the table and finish my spinach, which took me five minutes to chew.

So, coming back to my brother. His friend called him stupid because he deleted something on Minecraft. My brother does not like being called stupid. I have actually never met anyone who does! So he decided to leave. He is still friends with his "mate" and he made it clear to his mate never to call him stupid because he is not.

My brother was very clear to set his boundaries, and didn't let his friend's bad words hurt him. It is important to set your boundaries, and to know what you are and what you are not. What people say and think about you is not important.

CHAPTER 8

Successful Kids

*"Venture outside your comfort zone.
The rewards are worth it."*
Rapunzel (Tangled)

THE WORLD AROUND ME

Two years ago, my mother was doing research on kids in philanthropy. She was working on a project with Foundation for Young Australians and Jack Delosa.

I remember her spending so much time reading about programs around the world about young people in social change and Skyping a girl in the UK. The girl's mum had several meetings with her over the phone and was working for a program called 'UK Tenner'. Mum said that at that stage Sir Richard Branson was the patron of the program. What I like about UK Tenner is that kids are given £10, and they must find creative ways to grow the money and use it to create social change. This process teaches kids about caring for others and thinking about other people.

Kids who are involved in philanthropy care about our future, about our environment and about other kids who are struggling and who we can help.

When my Mum bought me the book Kidpreneur, by Matthew Toren and Adam Toren, I was very happy. It was signed for my sister, my brother and me. Matthew and Adam are brothers, who have set up several businesses and are very successful. They help young entrepreneurs with business skills like how to do research for your business in a modern way and some techniques for establishing and running a successful business.

I like reading such books as they help me understand the world around me. I also wanted to write a book. So I began writing down my talents and everything that I could do. Like most kids, my brother and sister and I thought about starting a lemonade stand

as a business. The problem was that our street is not very busy so not many people would stop by. Then we thought about things we could do on YouTube to share our ideas. That didn't go very well, but maybe in the near future we can try again.

Whatever business you decide to run, make sure you do your research. A lot of young people are doing great things in this country. Some are fundraising for the homeless, other are walking dogs, which I think might be a bit dangerous unless you know the dogs. But I would say if you are starting a business and you are my age, just make sure that you are safe and your first customers could be your family, friends or neighbours.

Before getting into business you need a business plan. It doesn't have to be a grown up business plan. Make one for yourself as a kid. Here is what I would recommend.

1. Write down your idea. What do you want to do or sell?

2. Work out what the start up cost will be.

3. Work out who your customers will be.

4. Think about how you would advertise the business.

The last one is easy. With social media, all you need to do is come up with some clever words and let other people share your posts and your ideas. Your success in your business depends on your customers, who can also help advertise it. If your customers are happy, you will be successful.

CHAPTER 9

Money Management

*"All our dreams can come true,
if we have the courage to pursue them."*
Walt Disney

It did take money, employees and a large team of artists to create Disneyland, but it all began with courage. It takes courage to begin the journey towards our dreams and courage to see them through.

I remember a few years ago when Mum bought me a piggy bank with a $20 sign on. I thought this would be great fun. What she didn't know was I wanted to grow my money. Yes you read right. I was only eight years old. I had to find ways of doing extra chores around the house to gain a few extra coins. I only wanted gold coins, as I could grow them much faster.

So, here is my master plan and I hope it works for you too. When I realised my piggy was full, I asked Mum to take me to the bank.

Of course my Mum, being very clever, came up with this line: "Give me your coins and I will transfer the money into your account". I said no. I wanted to go to the bank and have my own account.

She obliged, so we got my passport as a form of ID and went to the Commonwealth Bank where we opened up a Youthsaver account. What you may not know about this account is that it comes with its own Platybank moneybox (which looks like a platypus), which I use to save my gold coins.

I can say I'm pretty good at saving money. Most banks have programs for young people. It is very important to learn how to manage your money yourself. It is also important to know what kind of problems you want to solve when you grow up. If you don't know, that's ok too. One day you will!

Here are my tips:

1. Don't buy anything that you don't need. You money is best left in your account and that way it will grow.

2. Make sure that whatever you save will go into your account.

3. Only use money for the school canteen as a treat. I only buy canteen food when I feel like it and most of the time I will ask mum for $2 to buy something and get the rest of the food and drinks from the fridge. It's cheaper that way.

4. When shopping for clothes and shoes, make sure to get something that is good quality. This might cost you some money, but shop around. The last thing you want is to buy shoes three times a year because they are cheap and break easily.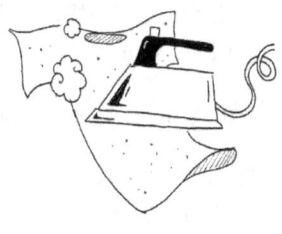

5. During Christmas and birthdays, ask your family not to buy you too many unnecessary gifts as most of them will end up in the bin after a few weeks. Ask them to put money in your account. Even $5 is enough.

6. Track your money. If you want to make a difference in the world, you can't do it while you are poor. Make some money and create a big business that will give jobs to a lot of people.

Now that I have shared with you my tips on how I save my money, I would like to hear from you. We can share some ideas on my Instagram account.

CONCLUSION

I hope that you have learned a lot from this book. The reason I wanted to write it is because great teachers like Jack Delosa, Dr John Demartini, my dad Dr Erik Beltz and my mum Nkandu Beltz have inspired me. I have also read lots of books about young people doing amazing things around the world. Imagine if we could all start doing something great for our communities? Reusing all the things we buy and sending as little as possible to land fill? We can reduce, reuse and recycle.

Imagine if you could pursue your business venture and help people.

Imagine if you could start that anti-bullying campaign at your school to help kids to be safe and teach others not to stand by when such things are happening.

Imagine what we could do by having so much fun and yet helping people at the same time, such as overseas in poor countries, or right here at home. You could fundraise for a school in Cambodia, so that kids there can get an education, or you could run a profitable business that employs a lot of people and helps them.

I hope this book has inspired you to do what you love.

ABOUT THE AUTHOR

My name is Claire. I believe that through this book I can change the world for the better. I know that the power of words spoken and written has a big effect on how the world can evolve. I have always loved writing, reading and maths so I figured I could write a good book, especially considering that I have written many stories at school and entered in writing competitions. I talked to my Mum about it and she agreed it was a great idea. Since she is the writer in my family, she gave me tips on how to make a story interesting and how to find inspiration when you're out of ideas. I don't have a lot of experience in writing about myself and public speaking but it's something I'd like to do.

My sister said something to me recently that inspired me. She said: "If you're feeling down, go to the North Pole, then you will be on top of the world." She meant what she said, but not literally.

Follow me on Instagram at **clairemalaikab**

Keep an eye on my blog **clairebeltz.com**

Claire Beltz

www.ingramcontent.com/pod-product-compliance
Lightning Source LLC
Chambersburg PA
CBHW070442010526
44118CB00014B/2157